field fare

Also by Valerie McLean

May Hill : Paintings and Drawings
Kilpeck and the Romanesque in Herefordshire
Edward Thomas : Paintings and drawings
www.valeriemclean.com

Copyright © 2023 Valerie McLean
ISBN 978 1 3999 5153 1

Typeface: Lato

British Library Cataloguing in Publication Data
A catalogue record for this book is available from the
British Library
Published by Sketchbook Publications 2023
Printed and bound by Orphans Press Ltd,
Herefordshire HR6 0LD

Walking Through the Seasons

By Valerie McLean

Dedicated to the memory of Roger Byron Hughes
(1943-2022)

Contents

Introduction
Ambulando Solvitur

This book is a record of my response to twelve of the many walks local to Ledbury, Newent, Dymock, Colwall and Eastnor, with a personal selection of poetry from poets who spent time in the area and took inspiration from the landscape. Several walks start from Ledbury and all are within ten miles of Ledbury Town. The walks are less than five miles long to allow time to stop and stare and maybe take photographs or draw in sketchbooks.

For me, walking is not a sport as it is for some people but a way to be outside in the natural world, alone or walking with others, while clearing the mind and refreshing the senses. When experiencing the world at a working pace and going back regularly to a particular footpath, I find a sense of belonging to a place rather than just passing through. Problems are solved and creative ideas are born. The idea for this book appeared in my mind while walking.

The illustrations are a collection of my artwork, not always a direct observational record but mostly sketchbook pages depicting an emotional response, made while out walking or from memory back in my studio in Ledbury. I find that a photograph can record a moment in time but a painting made later from the subconscious will record the lasting impact on the senses. Sometimes, I collect leaves and other natural treasures along the way to make drawings or prints in my studio.

All the walks can be taken in two to three hours when we have time on our hands to enjoy the countryside at a slow pace. I take walks at all times of the year but have chosen an appropriate month as a heading for each walk.

All the walks can be extended, connected or lead on to much longer routes and although most people have a phone to refer to, I recommend an O.S. Explorer 1:25000 map with Ledbury at its centre.

We are fortunate in having a railway station in Ledbury, which would have been used by Edward Thomas and family when they arrived in June 1914 to settle with other poets for one glorious summer near Ledbury and Dymock. One walk involves a seven minute train journey to Colwall. At the time of writing, the first week of the Daffodil Line bus service is underway, linking Ledbury Station with many villages and towns in the area, including Newent and Ross on Wye, allowing walkers to use cars less. (www.daffodilline.co.uk)

Said to be the nation's favourite poem, *Aldlestrop* was written on the battlefield by Edward Thomas as he remembered a stop on a train journey to Ledbury. The feelings around that moment of peace and beauty in June 1914, were recorded in his notebook at the time.

Adlestrop

Yes. I remember Adlestrop -
The name, because one afternoon
Of heat, the express-train drew up there
Unwontedly. It was late June.

The steam hissed. Someone cleared his throat.
No one left and no one came
On the bare platform. What I saw
Was Adlestrop—only the name

And willows, willow-herb, and grass,
And meadowsweet, and haycocks dry,
No whit less still and lonely fair
Than the high cloudlets in the sky.

And for that minute a blackbird sang
Close by, and round him, mistier,
Farther and farther, all the birds
Of Oxfordshire and Gloucestershire.

Edward Thomas

January

Eastnor Hill and the Eastnor Estate

This walk takes us on a gentle climb up Eastnor Hill, with views towards Eastnor and then a walk around parkland.

The large car park opposite Eastnor Castle has the attraction of a cabin selling quality drinks and snacks. We first make our way to the Grade 1 listed Church of St John the Baptist and take the sign posted path next to the church, then walk across the fields to climb Eastnor Hill for the views over Eastnor and beyond.
We retrace our steps and walk around the parkland of the Eastnor Estate, where we may see red deer and experience the spectacular view from the Eastnor Obelisk, erected as a memorial to the Somers Cocks family.
Access to this circular walk is through the gate at the back of the car park. We enjoy open views, small lakes, stately ancient trees, and on the far side of the park we find the path to climb up to the Obelisk. We retrace our steps down to the park and turning left we make our way back to the car park. Some of the paths in the parkland are tarmacked so are suitable for mobility scooters.

On Eastnor Knoll

Silent are the woods, and the dim green boughs are
Hushed in the twilight: yonder, in the path through
The apple orchard, is a tired plough-boy
Calling the cows home.

A bright white star blinks, the pale moon rounds, but
Still the red, lurid wreckage of the sunset
Smoulders in smoky fire, and burns on
The misty hill-tops.

Ghostly it grows, and darker, the burning
Fades into smoke, and now the gusty oaks are
A silent army of phantoms thronging
A land of shadows.

John Masefield

John Masefield's Tewkesbury Road refers to a route which runs through Eastnor, crosses the Malverns at Hollybush and then skirts Birtsmorton.

Tewkesbury Road

It is good to be out on the road, and going one knows not where,
 Going through meadow and village, one knows not whither nor why;
Through the grey light drift of the dust, in the keen cool rush of the air,
 Under the flying white clouds, and the broad blue lift of the sky;

And to halt at the chattering brook,in the tall green fern at the brink
 Where the harebell grows, and the gorse, and the foxgloves purple and white;
Where the shy-eyed delicate deer troop down to the pools to drink,
 When the stars are mellow and large at the coming on of the night.

O! to feel the warmth of the rain,and the homely smell of the earth,
 Is a tune for the blood to jig to, a joy past power of words;
And the blessed green comely meadows seem all a-ripple with mirth
 At the lilt of the shifting feet, and the dear wild cry of the birds.

John Masefield

walking talking looking

ambulando Solvitur

Saint Augustine — It is solved by walking

February

Frith Wood and back along orchards

This walk offers a mix of ancient woodland and views over orchards, the viaduct and open fields.

For this walk through woods and the return alongside orchards, we start from Ledbury Railway Station. From the station, we walk a few yards along the Bromyard Road, over the stile on the right where a track leads upwards alongside the orchard and through a gate. Here we turn left along the short tarmac path below Frith Wood House. (this is a right of way as confirmed by the Forestry Commision)

We now enter Frith Wood. During the winter, the trees give some shelter against inclement weather and on warm days, the trees cast a cool shade and a calm aura on this woodland path. Eventually a bench offers a view towards Wellington Heath. Further on, passing a sign - Peter Garrett Walk, we continue until a yellow arrow points to the parallel footpath that runs along the top of orchards and fields back to Ledbury.
We then pass ancient badger setts and in Winter the fieldfare and redwings feast on the windfalls. We come to a small quarry and nearer to Ledbury, the path takes us round an orchard, through a gate along the bottom of a charming cottage garden and across the fields to the path down to the road.

A longer walk can be enjoyed by including a loop with Wellington Heath

To take the longer walk, we do not turn off while on the Frith Wood path but continue on from the bench until we reach the road, then turn left and follow the road round into Wellington Heath. Along this quiet stretch of road we pass interesting restored buildings and impressive views towards Ledbury and beyond. For an extra detour, we will pass a gate next to the Hope End sign on our right giving access to a climb up onto Oyster Hill. However If we carry straight ahead, eventually we reach the sign to walk down the road to The Farmers Arms (closed Monday and Tuesday).

Opposite the pub, on the far side of the small recreation area a signpost points to a footpath guiding us through a metal gate, over fields, through a second gate and over a stream via a wooden bridge. Keeping close to the hedge, we then walk along the edge of fields upwards to join the lower path below Frith Wood, where we turn right and proceed on our way back to Ledbury as described previously.

Stopping by Woods on a Snowy Evening

Whose woods these are I think I know.
His house is in the village though;
He will not see me stopping here
To watch his woods fill up with snow.

My little horse must think it queer
To stop without a farmhouse near
Between the woods and frozen lake
The darkest evening of the year.

He gives his harness bells a shake
To ask if there is some mistake.
The only other sound's the sweep
Of easy wind and downy flake.

The woods are lovely, dark and deep,
But I have promises to keep,
And miles to go before I sleep,
And miles to go before I sleep.

Robert Frost

Thaw

Over the land freckled with snow half-thawed
The speculating rooks at their nests cawed
And saw from elm-tops, delicate as flower of grass,
What we below could not see, Winter pass.

The earth waking from winter sleep

We need to find our way

March

Dymock Poets Paths

The footpaths are named to remember the group known as the Dymock Poets who gathered, walked and talked in this area during the Summer of 1914, before W.W.1.

During the months of March and April, walking in the Dymock area is a special joy because of the profusion of wild daffodils in woods, fields and along lanes. In its heyday, the Great Western Railway offered special excursions to see and gather the daffodils, before they were protected as they are now.
Dymock is four miles south from Ledbury and was not always a small charming, rural village but a much larger rural trading area with markets and fairs centred on the wool industry, so there are many interesting historical buildings, including the ancient church of St Mary the Virgin and the parish owned Beaufort Arms pub.

I recommend parking in Dymock to visit the church inorder to view the permanent extensive exhibition about the Dymock Poets and a full range of leaflets to guide walkers round the many footpaths.

The members of the group were : Robert Frost, Edward Thomas, Wilfred Gibson, Lascelles Abercrombie, Rupert Brooke and John Drinkwater and others visited, including Ivor Gurney.

Sean Street tells the story in his book *The Dymock Poets*, of how writers with international reputations gathered here just before the outbreak of W.W. 1

"A respected Georgian journal was published as a cottage industry, and men and women sought an idyll of Dream England, as if they knew that this might be their last chance"

My favourite walking area is a few miles from the church. So, I suggest driving to Gwen and Vera's Field Nature Reserve, parking at nearby Shaw Common, to start exploring Greenaway's Wood, which leads on to Betty Daws Wood. We can then retrace our steps or walk back along the road to Shaw Common.

As well as wild daffodils, the habitat hosts a vast range of plants including bluebells and wood anemones.

To reach these nature reserves, we find Kempley Road, a short way down from the green in front of the church on the opposite side of the road. We drive left into this road and left again, then carry on eventually taking a right fork in the road and cross the motorway. To our right we can park at Shaw Common and to our left we can find Gwen and Vera's field and the Nature Reserves.

Lascelles Abercrombie, composed *Ryton Firs* as he remembered the beautiful woods, felled for pit props in the Welsh mines. I have selected a fragment from the long poem.

From Dymock, Kempley, Newent, Bromesberrow,
Redmarley, all the meadowland daffodils seem
Running in golden tides to Ryton Firs,
To make the knot of steep little wooded hills
Their brightest show: O bella età de l'oro!
Now I breathe you again, my woods of Ryton:
Not only golden with your daffodil light
Lying in pools on the loose dusky ground
Beneath the larches, tumbling in broad rivers
Down sloping grass under the cherry trees
And birches: but among your branches clinging
A mist of that Ferrara-gold I first
Loved in the easy hours you made so green

Lascelles Abercrombie

24

April

Ledbury to Eastnor via Coneygree Wood

This walk takes us through historic woodland with remarkable plants, birdlife and ancient tree species then through fields to the village of Eastnor.

The walk starts in the centre of Ledbury, in the churchyard of the 14th century St Michaels and All Angels Parish Church. A historic passageway called Cabbage Lane leads from the Southern side of the churchyard out onto the main Worcester Road. Here we turn left, passing the police station and after a short distance cross the road to the steps into Coneygree woods. John Masefield referred to this spot as having "a pretty road-side brook under a wall where toad-flax grew".

I find the climb up through the stoney gullet into this quite dense magical wood to be memorable in so many ways and in all seasons. The variety of tree species including the wild service tree and small leaf lime indicate ancient origins.

The route all the way to Eastnor is clearly indicated by the impact of the thousands of previous walkers. We cross a wide Forestry path then continue climbing, eventually passing through two gates and come to a level open area known as Dead Woman's Thorn (Sometimes called Dead Man's Thorn).

A section of John Masefield's famous long poem *The Ever Lasting Mercy* was set at this location, describing a fight between two poachers.

From here we continue on through a third gate until we are rewarded with a splendid view across the fields to the Malvern Hills and down into Eastnor. We can find a different route back by turning to the right by Eastnor School, passing the Pottery and following the blue bridle path signs back over the fields reaching a short section of the Gloucester Road. Turn right to Ledbury, shielded by a row of shrubs and trees. However, I prefer to retrace my steps and experience the route back through Coneygree Woods. The name Coneygree originates from coney to mean a rabbit warren and a wild rabbit stew would have been a popular tasty nutritious meal in the past.

Rupert Brooke was a member of The Dymock Poets and I have included his famous war sonnet, *The Soldier* because this poem made him famous, also drawing attention to *New Numbers*, the periodical published during the group's time in the Dymock and Leddington area. The poem reflects the patriotic, romantic mood of most of the country at the start of W.W.1.

The Soldier

If I should die, think only this of me:
  That there's some corner of a foreign field
That is for ever England. There shall be
  In that rich earth a richer dust concealed;
A dust whom England bore, shaped, made aware,
  Gave, once, her flowers to love, her ways to roam,
A body of England's, breathing English air,
  Washed by the rivers, blest by suns of home.

And think, this heart, all evil shed away,
  A pulse in the eternal mind, no less
  Gives somewhere back the thoughts by England given;
Her sights and sounds; dreams happy as her day;
  And laughter, learnt of friends; and gentleness,
    In hearts at peace, under an English heaven.

Rupeert Brooke died on April 23rd 1915 and is buried on the Greek island of Skyros.

From inside the wood

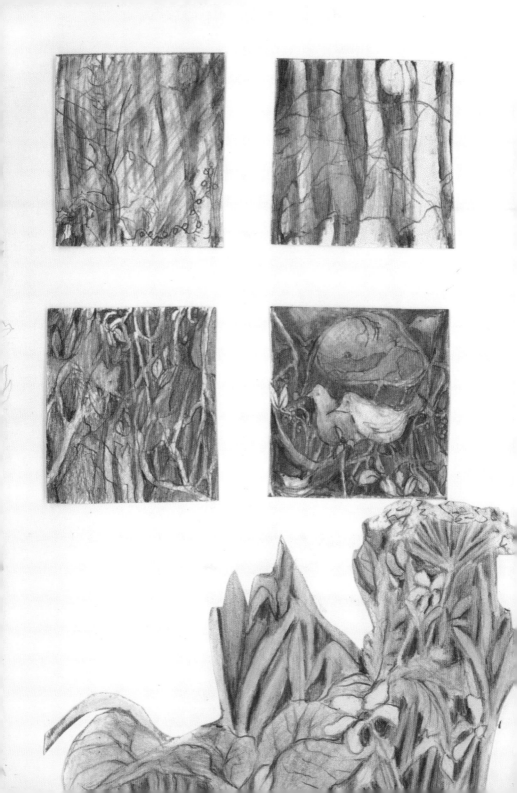

Bradwell Knoll

Thursday 8th April

Blue
Brandon

May

Green Lane and Dog Hill Wood

This walk around a wooded hill offers views with a stroll along an ancient trackway and back along uneven, winding paths.

Above Ledbury, Dog Hill Wood is bordered on one side by an old packhorse route called Green Lane which must have been widened and surfaced in earlier times to allow for horse drawn vehicles and the drovers bringing animals to Ledbury market.
Starting from the Market House in the centre of Ledbury, we walk up the cobbled Church Lane towards the ancient Church of St Michaels and All Angels which is open for visitors to view the treasures within and enjoy the reflective space.
From the churchyard we walk through the walled garden , or along the adjacent walled pathway up the road to the shallow flight of steps that lead eventually to the wide stoney path on the right known as Green Lane.

There is an open area on the right with splendid views of Ledbury, towards May Hill and Marcle Ridge.

Walking upwards along the path we pass gnarled tree roots, ivy clad crumbling stone walls spouting ferns and many varieties of flora. There are several seats to rest and enjoy bird song while enjoying views towards the Eastnor Obelisk, British Camp and the Malvern Hills.

Along the way I find a feeling of walking in the past, imagining all the people and animals who have used this path; an echo of previous lives.

At the junction with Cut Throat lane and Knapp Lane we wind our way back over the hill, under the overhanging trees whilst negotiating fallen tree stumps and steep tracks, back to the lower path where we turn left to return to the church. For an easier stroll back we retrace our steps or we could continue on over the road to connect with another footpath.

A longer walk from the end of Green Lane returning via the Upper Hall Farm Quarry is featured for the June walk and another walk returning via Bradlow Knoll for the July walk.

Many Green Lanes have been walked into the land elsewhere. This poem was written by Edward Thomas as he remembered walking along a Green Lane in Foxfield.

The Lane

Some day, I think, there will be people enough
In Froxfield to pick all the blackberries
Out of the hedges of Green Lane, the straight
Broad lane where now September hides herself
In bracken and blackberry, harebell and dwarf gorse.
Today, where yesterday a hundred sheep
Were nibbling, halcyon bells shake to the sway
Of waters that no vessel ever sailed...
It is a kind of spring: the chaffinch tries
His song. For heat it is like summertoo.
This might be winter's quiet. While the glint
Of hollies dark in the swollen hedge lasts -
One mile - and those bells ring, little I know
Or heed if time be still the same, until
The lane ends and once more all is the same.

Edward Thomas

The Lane was one of the last poems Edward Thomas wrote, in December 1916 a few weeks before embarking for France with his artillery unit.

June

Green Lane to Upper Hall Quarry and Grassland

After walking along Green Lane, as described in the May walk, there is an opportunity to return via a protected Site of Special Scientific Interest including a meadow glorious in Summer with wild flowers.

After crossing the road from Green Lane and walking up past the gate for Bradlow Knoll on the left, we keep following the road round bearing right and then turning right at the junction and walking down to the next junction. On the way early in the year, the banks provide a good show of snowdrops and where there are gaps in the hedges, we catch glimpses of the Malvern Hills.

The stile opposite is a gateway to the Upper Hall Farm Quarry and Grassland Area and in Summer we step into a medieval meadow of wildflowers, including orchids. We turn right and walk right around the field, keeping next to the hedge and ignoring the gate in the corner. Eventually, following the hedge and bearing to the right, we find a larger gate and the route to continue through this S.S.S.I. area. About half way along the path we pass a disused quarry , exposing the earth's ancient history. I find this area to be a mixture of history, geology and industry as well as wildlife.

As we leave the site bordered by a traditional layered hedge, we turn left, finding a narrow footpath down the road on the right just before the junction. This footpath guides us back to Green Lane and Ledbury Town.

A Blade of Grass

Cool, it touched my warm hand,
infant splendor of newness,
smelling of fresh cut summer lawns,
succulent vegetables, birth gladness.

How fine it was, this one blade,
until the warmth of my hand wilted it,
twisting, curling it into a limp poor thing,
Oh sin!

Jane Amherst

Mid June on Chase End Hill

There are explosions on umbrella'd leaves
wet rain on warm earth.
Powerful rays spotlight my path
And I am washed by wet leaves as I pass.

A smell of green freshness permeates skin,
I breath deeply,
then hear it, a beautiful hymn from
a thrush's notes, in triple calls,
practising scales as night still falls.
Up up he goes to glorious heights,
thrilling air with purest sound,
while far below, on muddy ground,
trees stand, rustling jubilation.

Jane Amherst

Jane Amherst's poems were inspired by long solitary
walks on the hills around Ledbury and Hollybush.

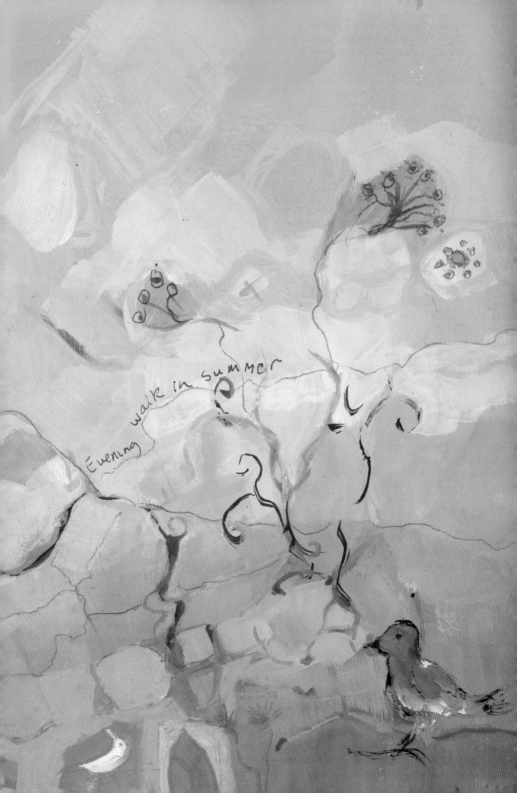

Evening walk in summer

July

Onward to Bradlow Knoll

Continuing from the end of Green Lane, this longer walk involves an exhilarating climb up to Bradlow Knoll and a walk through an enchanted small avenue of trees before descending to Frith wood and returning to Ledbury.

After walking along Green Lane (described in the May walk), we cross the road and walk a couple of hundred yards upwards, along West Hill to find a sign-posted path then go through the gate on the left. Then a challenging steady plod up the hill will reward us with a rather special memorial seat to rest and enjoy the view from the highest point above Ledbury.

Near to the seat is the entrance to a section of Frith Wood with the feel of an enchanted world. There are signs of ancient human activity with boundary markers, mounds and ditches. We walk upwards along the path worn into the hill and come across the sign - Bradlow Knoll. Here we turn left down the woodland path, then turn left again on the wide path back towards Ledbury.

Edward Thomas wrote *It was upon on* 22nd June 1916 at
Hare Camp where he was a map reading instructor.
Thomas was uncertain what his next step should be,
though he increasingly felt compelled to go to France.

It was upon

It was upon a July evening.
At a stile I stood, looking along a path
Over the country by a second Spring
Drenched perfect green again. 'The lattermath
Will be a fine one.' So the stranger said,
A wandering man. Albeit I stood at rest,
Flushed with desire I was. The earth outspread,
Like meadows of the future, I possessed.

And as an unaccomplished prophecy
The stranger's words, after the interval
Of a score years, when the fields are by me
Never to be recrossed, now I recall
This July eve, and question, wondering,
What of the lattermath of this hoar Spring?

Edward Thomas

The Dark Forest

Dark is the forest and deep, and overhead
Hang stars like seeds of light
In vain, though not since they were sown was bred
Anything more bright.

And evermore mighty multitudes ride
About, nor enter in;
Of the other multitudes that dwell inside
Never yet was one seen.

The forest foxglove is purple, the marguerite
Outside is gold and white,
Nor can those that pluck either blossom greet
The others, day or night.

Edward Thomas

The earth out spread,   like

eadows of the future, I possessed

Apple walking for Heath

August

Ledbury Town Trail

This quiet tree lined footpath allows a traffic free walk from the railway station to the centre of Ledbury and the option of a circular route back by the River Leadon

This footpath cuts through housing developments and is a successful linear wildlife habitat, constructed on the original route of the canal which was in turn replaced by the railway. John Masefield's childhood was spent at a house in the Homend called The Knapp and in his book *Grace before Ploughing*, he recorded his memories of the activities on the canal.

"The canal, horses, people and wonder, made the great romance of every day and the beauty of some of its reaches I can never forget"
"I have lively memories of the woman steering with her most becoming head-dress of a milkmaid's cap flapping on her cheeks, and the husband ahead minding the horse, and often singing, or knitting, or flinging words over his shoulder to his wife"

I have witnessed so much wildlife on this sometimes busy track where children walk to school and people walk their dogs. Walking regularly into town, I have heard the full range of bird song, also woodpeckers, owls, as well as domestic quarrels up high in the noisy rookery. I once observed a clever crow with a twig in its beak, poking an opening in a tree to find any larvae or other titbits. In very cold Winters, the redwings swoop in over the recreation ground.

Very early one morning in summer I met a badger ambling along and on another very early walk, a fox descended down into the overgrown garden of the empty house next door to where I live.
The pathway continues on after we cross a narrow bridge reaching the recreation ground and then we cross a road onto a quiet, more shady section of the Town Trail..
Eventually, after crossing a road we use a shorter footpath and cross the very busy Ledbury by-pass to reach the Riverside Park.

The riverside walk is a delight, especially in Summer when the trees are in leaf and so shut out traffic noise. We eventually reach the well laid out paths of the end section of the park and can walk back along the road to the Station.

The Glory

The glory of the beauty of the morning, -
The cuckoo crying over the untouched dew;
The blackbird that has found it, and the dove
That tempts me on to something sweeter than love;
White clouds ranged even and fair as new-mown hay;
The heat, the stir, the sublime vacancy
Of sky and meadow and forest and my own heart: -
The glory invites me, yet it leaves me scorning
All I can ever do, all I can be,
Beside the lovely of motion, shape, and hue,
The happiness I fancy fit to dwell
In beauty's presence. Shall I now this day
Begin to seek as far as heaven, as hell,
Wisdom or strength to match this beauty, start
And tread the pale dust pitted with small dark drops,
In hope to find whatever it is I seek

Edward Thomas

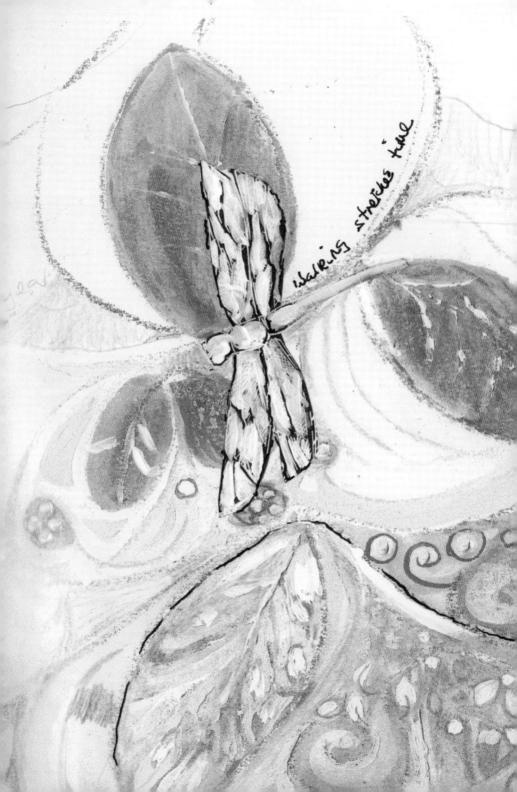

watching stretches time

September

A walk from Colwall to Ledbury

After a short train journey we walk along quiet country roads, around a community orchard, through peaceful countryside back to Ledbury.

Ledbury Train Station is the starting point for a seven minute train journey to Colwall Village which in the past was a centre for orchards and fruit growing. An hour or two may be spent following the Colwall Orchard Heritage Trail around the village (trail map available from The Post Office).

To walk back to Ledbury from Colwall Station, we cross over from The Colwall Park Hotel, follow the road along Stone Drive and turn left along Old Church Road. Entering the Village Garden, we walk next to the hedge parallel to the road, eventually reaching the gate to Brookmead Community orchard, rich in wildlife and open for all to enjoy. We follow the path round to the right, through a gate and across a bridge over a stream. We exit further along the road and come to a bend where we turn onto a sign-posted footpath on the right.

Keeping close to the hedge on the left we follow the path and eventually turn left to see the ancient Church of St.James the Great in the distance which was the centre of the village before the railway arrived. There is an interesting well preserved 16th century Ale House near the church

Turn right through the churchyard and follow the road ahead to a junction. Turn left, passing first one then a second gatehouse to Hope End House where Elizabeth Barrett Browning spent her early years. Reaching an area called Petty France, we turn right along a footpath into Frith Wood and turn left to Ledbury, or follow signs walking along the road to return via Green Lane and Dog Hill Wood.

Patience taught by Nature

'O DREARY life,' we cry, ' O dreary life ! '
And still the generations of the birds
Sing through our sighing, and the flocks and herds
Serenely live while we are keeping strife
With Heaven's true purpose in us, as a knife
Against which we may struggle ! Ocean girds
Unslackened the dry land: savannah-swards
Unweary sweep, hills watch unworn, and rife
Meek leaves drop year]y from the forest-trees
To show, above, the unwasted stars that pass
In their old glory: O thou God of old,
Grant me some smaller grace than comes to these !--
But so much patience as a blade of grass
Grows by, contented through the heat and cold.

Elizabeth Barret Browning

Aurora Leigh

Aurora Leigh is an epic poem/novel by Elizabeth Barrett Browning in 1856 and contains references to her childhood spent in the countryside at Hope End.

As poets use, the skies, the clouds, the fields
The happy violets from the roads
The primroses run down to, carrying gold;
'Twixt dripping ash-boughs,—hedgerows all alive
With birds and gnats and large white butterflies,
Which look as if the May-flower had caught life
And palpitated forth upon the wind;
Hills, vales, woods, netted in a silver mist,
Farms, granges, doubled up among the hills;
And cattle grazing in the watered vales,
And cottage-chimneys smoking from the woods,
And cottage-gardens smelling everywhere,
Confused with the smell of orchards. 'See,' I said,
'And see! is God not with us on the earth?
And shall we put him down by aught we do?
Who says there 's nothing for the poor and vile
Save poverty and wickedness?
 behold!'
And ankle-deep in English grass I leaped
And clapped my hands, and called all very fair.

a walk through fields of buttercups where poets

lked and talked

...ing, and ... ...ly wit...
...om other bo... ...ing ...ak...
by repeating what...se... ...of ... ...adi...
...oughly ex... ...e... ...i... ...p...
...rom ...arag... ...a ...nol... ...ente...
...it ...
...other book.

...author... ...d... or
...d, is free... ...t...
...lave o... ...a

...ed with the ...ount of ...ten...
...to an... ...ent d...
...t of ... ...it...
...d, in... ...sequen...
...ngn...ss...
...no...h...

...and by...
...es of conviction...
while ...conceived...
...opy...
Think while walking, wa... ...le...
...e light ...s... the body...
...ace...

outside

o judge .... music.
the foot. If .... wish ....
.. rk the r...... gn. A.
on to light ...... sic depress ....
respect: it ..ke.... forgets how ... a ..... Wor..
still i ...... g. arns t.is way and .ha. .is ir..
... .aste. ...... agner, as Nietzsche ....

October

Oyster Hill

A chance to enjoy a gentle walk through the landscape where Elizabeth Barrett Browning lived and roamed for the first twenty six years of her life, then a climb to a magnificent view towards Wales

My usual parking place is near the Parish Church at Wellington Heath, on the outskirts of Ledbury. At this road junction, a beautiful but dying oak tree has been given a new life with intricate carvings of birds and other creatures from the local countryside and is crowned with a red kite in flight. If we are lucky, as we walk over the hill, we may experience the imposing presence of swooping and gliding red kites identified by their wide wing span and forked tails.
From this point, we walk up the road, passing wonderful views on our right towards Ledbury and beyond until we reach the sign to Hope End House
To the left, a gate leads across a meadow and following traces of previous walkers, we gradually find our way to the summit of the hill and the glorious views over the villages and fields towards the Welsh hills in the distance.

On the way we pass beautifully restored buildings, a walled garden and as we climb towards the summit of the hill, a glimpse through the trees of the present Hope End House that replaced the original mansion of Indian Gothic design. This is the area where Elizabeth Barrett Browning spent her early life, often riding or walking in the countryside.

After a rest on a convenient seat we continue down the other side of the hill, turning left, joining a stony track bordered by ancient hedges and trees, eventually turning left onto Raycombe Lane and the route back to Wellington Heath and the carved tree. The nearby church yard is a pleasure to visit for the views at all times of the year and wild flowers, including orchids in Summer.

There are constant reminders in Elizabeth Barrett
Browning's writing of her early life at Hope End.

The Autumn

Go, sit upon the lofty hill,
And turn your eyes around,
Where waving woods and waters wild
Do hymn an autumn sound.
The summer sun is faint on them --
The summer flowers depart --
Sit still -- as all transform'd to stone,
Except your musing heart.

How there you sat in summer-time,
May yet be in your mind;
And how you heard the green woods sing
Beneath the freshening wind.
Though the same wind now blows around,
You would its blast recall;
For every breath that stirs the trees,
Doth cause a leaf to fall.

Oh! like that wind, is all the mirth
That flesh and dust impart:
We cannot bear its visitings,
When change is on the heart.
Gay words and jests may make us smile,
When Sorrow is asleep;
But other things must make us smile,
When Sorrow bids us weep!

Elizabeth Barrett Browning

— misty and — such colours

me . . and there is no possible alternative here. Also, the
cold cannot be shut out so effectually ~~and~~ to operate injuri-
ously, *for*, said Dr. Chambers, you are not to think this, merely
nervous weakness—though you are very nervous!—it is in
great part from the muscles covering the lungs being affected
by the cold air . . and nothing but warm air is a remedy to
it. He left me in great spirits about myself and about what
Pisa is to do for me—and I have since heard nothing but good
of the place and climate. The sea is to do good too, I under-
stand . . and I am not fearing it in any way. At the same
time I am in very doubtful spirits—very agitated and full of
sad thoughts . . from many causes . . which I cannot enter
now. You shall hear from me my . . dearest Miss Mitford
before I leave England—and over the Alps, my letters shall
fly by as many a drove as shall be . . . the considerations
of postage. Dr. Chambers named . . the earliest time of
. . . the coming . . time to England, . . . ing Pisa—and in the
. . . . gave any kind . . . . et to lose me, must
. . . . my bodily weakness
. . . . sight of me . . . . ed out on the sofa
. . . . to the child . . . Whereas on light
. . . . I sh . . . . perhaps out of the . . . . very day in . . . .
. . . . day that it does . . . . and able . . . .
. . . . with gladder . . . . . . fonder thought.
do not . . . . . . me my . . . . . friend—do . . .
. . . . . . for the p . . . . now) I should . . . .
. . . . to have . . . . . . so as . . . . . . able to think of . . .
. . . . own l . . . . and . . . you have been . . . .
. . . . yon his . . . . been persuading m .
. . . . looking . . . . life before . . . . . .
it . . . . am looking much
bett . . . . though still . . . . . . ing
. . . . and . . . . . ing white with . .
exertion . An . . . . the us . . . . . eans of growing
strong, you . . . . ers persu . . . . desiring that . . . .
should live ch . . . . milk and vegeta . . . and eschew . . . .
'strong meats and drinks' of the strong . . . . which proves th . .
he has som . . . . in the face of . . . .

I will w . . . . Mr. Kenyon's . . . . . . on the flying . . .
my letter—but he . . . in town only for a day, and you . . . . .

likely to find him immediately. This is his time for 'flitting'
you know! His goodness and kindness to me have been
inexpressible as the___ ___ past speaking of,—I cannot __ to
___ ___ ___ . . in ___ ___ence to this Pisa-business. I can
only be grateful all ___ ___ ays of my life to him—be the life
shorter or longer !

And now, no mo__. O__y ___ __ shall hear again. Oh no,
no—your affection for___ ___ should not draw you into such a
toil . . even if it were ___ble for you to go to Italy, which
I know it is n__ ___ ___ shall be 'back again in a moment'
you know___ ___ __te lightly when my spirits are as
they are ___ ___ __s how!

___ ___ __y God bles__ ___ __ur E B B.

___ my compan___ ___ __pe for too
___ __aps and it is ___ __tled. You

though E B ___ a July 18, 1845, ___ ___ding her to
__ __r Malt__ ___ ___ __not until ___ __t there is a
___ the Pisa ___ __ __ber 3, D__ ___ __as given his
full ___ Pisa ___ __ 8, there is a disc__ ___ __mers, and
first ___ me___ ___ __ad silence of Papa's ___ ___ __7,
E B ___ ___ __ P__ __ __ S__ teml___ ___ __en
aga__ ___ we__re __ ___ __ positio__ __ __ __op-
teml___ ___ __hs have been tak__ ___ __lta stea__ __ __ __ch
the 3 ___ October. On October__ __ __whole p__ __is fina__ y
aband___

[50 Wimpole ___ _et]
Saturday, 1 September 45]

Eve___ Miss Mitford, ___ I thank you for __ pretty
translat___ thoughts of ___ __or so I like to consider it.
It is ___ __en wi__ __ ___ __w. How kind, and how
I that ___

W___ ___ __five ___ ___ __denes—(I enclose
the or ___ ___ __m __ ___ __rother's __in?
___ ___ __uld __y, __ am __ __uch in anxiety and
tribu___ __le ___ __a__ __ It is all uncertain whether I shall __
or no ___ __ __an__ __untime I am vexed out of patience.
___ __ __ __er is stooping through __ wet and damp

Into the Landscape rather than through it

November

Hollybush Common

A walk round an open landscape offering views over rolling hills and open common grassland as we pass trees dripping with mistletoe, and then rest by a small picturesque lake.

All Saints Church at Hollybush is our starting point where there is ample room to park. On the east side of the church we turn to the right and take in the views toward the North and the Malvern Hills and make our way along the top of the Common. We may share the space with sheep grazing, the occasional horse and rider as well as fellow walkers. Eventually a grassy track appears and we start losing height until we reach a flat area of the Common and cross a stream via a small wooden bridge, carved with the name of that part of the common - Coombe Green. We then follow the track round to the left.

We continue on to find the lake crossing via the stepping stones to be greeted by geese and other wildfowl and a perfect place to rest and watch the wildlife. Walking by the lake we then start walking upward until guided by the sight of the church in the distance.

Walking with others often allows special friendships to flourish. People walked long distances in the past and we know from Robert Frost's notebook that this poem was written after a very long walk with Edward Thomas. They walked from Leddington, near Ledbury, to Bromsberrow Heath then via Hollybush to Castlemorton Common, then to British Camp, through Eastnor Park back to Leddington. The Poem, *Iris by Night* describes a moonbow that seemed to encircle them at the end of the walk and this was felt to be a symbol of their friendship.

Iris by Night

One misty evening, one another's guide,
We two were groping down a Malvern side
The last wet fields and dripping hedges home.
There came a moment of confusing lights,
Such as according to belief in Rome
Were seen of old at Memphis on the heights
Before the fragments of a former sun
Could concentrate anew and rise as one.
Light was a paste of pigment in our eyes.
And then there was a moon and then a scene
So watery as to seem submarine;
In which we two stood saturated, drowned.
The clover-mingled rowan on the ground
Had taken all the water it could as dew,
And still the air was saturated too,
Its airy pressure turned to water weight.

Then a small rainbow like a trellis gate,
A very small moon-made prismatic bow,
Stood closely over us through which to go.
And then we were vouchsafed a miracle
That never yet to other two befell
And I alone of us have lived to tell.
A wonder! Bow and rainbow as it bent,
Instead of moving with us as we went
(To keep the pots of gold from being found),
It lifted from its dewy pediment
Its two mote-swimming many-colored ends
And gathered them together in a ring.
And we stood in it softly circled round
From all division time or foe can bring
In a relation of elected friends.

Robert Frost

glorious spring light

December

May Hill

The distinctive silhouette of May Hill can be seen from hundreds of miles away and with a height of almost 1000 feet, the views are breathtaking. The colours of flowers, plants, trees and mosses are vibrant all year round, even in winter when holly and ivy have their moment.

Although May Hill is ten miles from Ledbury, I have included this destination in this book because it is a constant presence during most of the other walks and has inspired many local poets and artists.

After driving into Newent from Ledbury via Dymock, I suggest turning first right onto Watery Lane and following the road until the sign for the Yew Tree pub (which is now a house). There are several footpaths to the summit from here, or further on through May Hill Village. After a climb through the woods, eventually a gate leads onto the large area of grassland where the famous pine trees are waiting. Sometimes wild horses graze, helping to keep the vegetation in check.

I find May Hill is somewhere to linger and experience the peace and wonder of a place where people gather at significant times of the year such as Easter for a dawn service, on May Day or on special occasions when a beacon may be lit.

As part of my art practice, I make journeys to sacred buildings and I find special areas of countryside like May Hill draw pilgrims in the way that medieval churches do. In the darkest months of the year we need to seek out opportunities to rejoice in natural light whenever we can so a walk to the summit of a hill can bring a feeling of exhilaration and wellbeing especially in Winter.
If we walk away from the trees, clockwise around the edge of the summit we can see far over Herefordshire to the Severn Estuary, Gloucestershire, the Black mountains, and the Forest of Dean. We can then continue to make our way round and retrace our steps. The Daffodil line bus will take walkers from Ledbury to Gorsley and/or Kilcot for alternative routes to May Hill and easy access to Dymock woods.
The shape of the trees seen from afar has changed over the years. John Masefield, as a child saw the clump of tree as a giant ploughman and wrote:

> "I've marked the may hill ploughman stay
> There on his hill, day after day
> Driving his team against the sky,
> While men and women die."

Words (over leaf) was composed by Edward Thomas after walking on May Hill with his friend, John Haines.

Words

Out of us all
That make rhymes
Will you choose
Sometimes -
As the winds use
A crack in a wall
Or a drain,
Their joy or their pain
To whistle through -
Choose me,
You English words?

I know you:
You are light as dreams,
Tough as oak,
Precious as gold,
As poppies and corn,
Or an old cloak:
Sweet as our birds
To the ear,
As the burnet rose
In the heat
Of Midsummer:
Strange as the races
Of dead and unborn:
Strange and sweet
Equally,
And familiar,
To the eye,
As the dearest faces
That a man knows,
And as lost homes are:
But though older far

Than oldest yew, -
As our hills are, old, -
Worn new
Again and again:
Young as our streams
After rain:
And as dear
As the earth which you prove
That we love.

Make me content
With some sweetness
From Wales
Whose nightingales
Have no wings, -
From Wiltshire and Kent
And Herefordshire, -
And the villages there, -
From the names, and the things
No less.

Let me sometimes dance
With you,
Or climb
Or stand perchance
In ecstasy,
Fixed and free
In a rhyme,
As poets do.

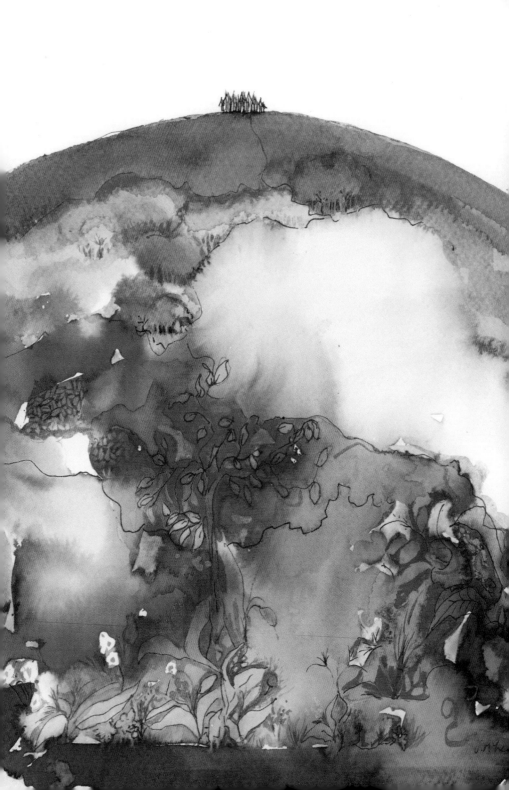

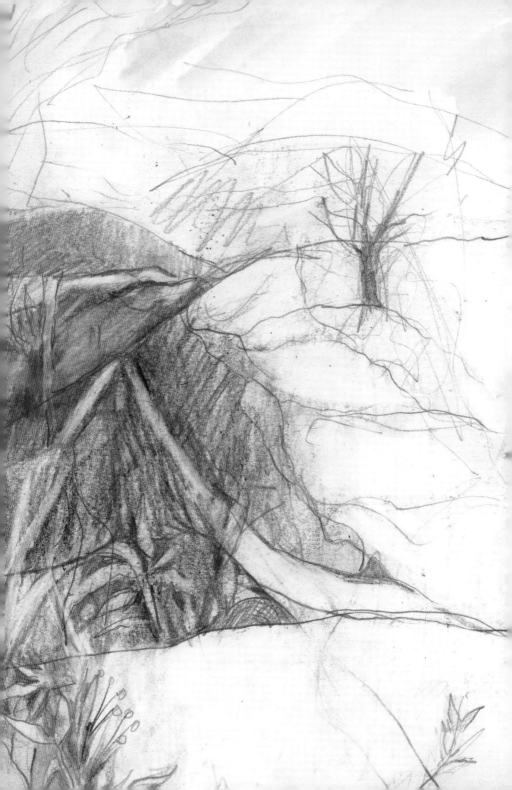

Rhytar Firs
are alive again

all around the knoll on days of quietest air
secrets are being told

List of artwork

List of Poems

Acknowledgements

Thank you to everyone who helped shape this book, which is dedicated to the memory of my partner, Roger Hughes, who introduced me to regular country walks thirty years ago. Roger bravely continued to attempt to walk until M.S. took away his mobility.

I am one of a gang of five artists who take monthly walks, exploring the countryside around Ledbury, Newent, Dymock, Eastnor and Colwall. So thanks to Philip, Tony, Jenny and Angie for keeping this ritual going for so many years. Thanks to Diane for many shared walks, particularly our favourite climb over May Hill.

Many friends and family have been my companions on many walks including, Andrea, Stuart, Sally, Ellen, Alex, Jess and Harvey, Hal, Ace and Vivienne.

Thank you to my son Stuart who has been very supportive, especially with his specialist I.T. skills. Thanks to Tony Bateman for his map reading skills and drawing the map. Thanks to Jackie Tweedale for information about matters relating to John Masefield. Thank you to the Society of Authors for permission to quote from John Masefield's *Tewksbury Road* and *Eastnor Knoll*. Thanks to Jeff Cooper for permission to quote from Lascelles Abercrombie's *Ryton Firs*. Thanks to Jonathan Lumby for permission to include *A blade of Grass and Mid June on Chase End Hill* by Jane Amherst. Thanks to Amanda and Ledbury Library staff for cheerfully providing such a good service. Thanks to Douglas McLean for help and advice on publishing. Thank you to Lindsay at Ledbury Books and Maps, Ledbury for sharing her vast knowledge of publishing and bookselling. Lindsay suggested approaching Orphans Publishing. I am grateful to the team at Orphans for their excellent service.

Bibliography

Jane Amherst, *The Winding Lane*, Margot Miller, 2021

Paul Binding, *An Endless Quiet valley, A Reappraisal of John Masefield*, Longston Press 1998

Barbara Dennis, *The Hope End Years*, Poetry Wales Press Ltd. 1996

Philip Errington (Ed) *Sea-Fever: Selected Poems of John Masefield*, Carcanet Press Ltd 2005

Frederic Gros *A philosophy of Walking*, Verso, 2014

Linda Hart, *Once they lived in Gloucestershire*, Green Branch Press, 2000

Jonathan Lumby (Ed) *Poems and Paintings of the Malvern Hills*, Logaston Press 2014

Edna Longley (Ed) *Edward Thomas,, The Annotated Collected Poems*, BloodaxeBooks, 2008

John Masefield, *Grace Before Ploughing*, Heinemann 1996

Shane O'Mara, *In praise of Walking*, Penguin 2019

Christopher Somerville, *The January Man*, Transworld Publishers 2017

Sean Street, *The Dymock Poets*, Poetry Wales Ltd. 1994

Hugh Warwick, *Linescapes*, Penguin Books, 2017

Philip Weaver, *A dictionary of Herefordshire Biography* Logaston Press 2015

Websites

browningsociety.org
www.daffodilline.co.uk
www.dymockpoets.org.uk
earthheritagetrust.org
ledburypoetry.org.uk

The Road not Taken

Two roads diverged in a yellow wood,
And sorry I could not travel both
And be one traveler, long I stood
And looked down one as far as I could
To where it bent in the undergrowth;

Then took the other, as just as fair,
And having perhaps the better claim,
Because it was grassy and wanted wear;
Though as for that the passing there
Had worn them really about the same,

And both that morning equally lay
In leaves no step had trodden black.
Oh, I kept the first for another day!
Yet knowing how way leads on to way,
I doubted if I should ever come back.

I shall be telling this with a sigh
Somewhere ages and ages hence:
Two roads diverged in a wood, and I—
I took the one less traveled by,
And that has made all the difference.

Robert Frost

Hazel Nuts

poor little dead blackbird

an ending is also a beginning